Arizona DUI Guide, From Arrest to Trial

Arizona DUI Guide, From Arrest to Trial

Things You Need to Know

Nathan D. Leonardo

Nathan D. Leonardo
Leonardo Law Offices, PLLC

(520) 314-4125

www.TucsonDUILawyers.net

ISBN: 1535548851
ISBN 13: 9781535548854

PREFACE

I f you are reading this book, there's a good chance that you have just experienced one of the worst nights of your life. You may have been arrested for DUI and then let go, or you may have been booked into jail and just recently released. Either way, you're probably scared, or at least worried, about what fate awaits you in court. You may be embarrassed, or you may be angry, but know that you're not alone.

Every year in Arizona, thousands of people from all walks of life are charged with DUI. You might be surprised how many of your neighbors and people in your area have gone through exactly what you're going through right now. You should know that your situation is not hopeless; it is possible to navigate your way through the DUI minefield and get to the other side relatively unscathed.

The good news is that, by having bought this book, you are one step ahead of most people in your situation. You have already taken the first of several steps that can lead to a successful outcome in your case.

I must admit: I spent the first several years of my legal career prosecuting cases like yours. A lot of these cases were justified, but I also saw many bad cases result in people being convicted when they probably shouldn't have been. The sheer volume of DUI cases being processed was staggering, and it still is.

It has now gotten to the point where it has become difficult to select a jury for a DUI trial because so many of the prospective jurors have

DUI convictions. These are regular working people who, for the most part, are productive and law-abiding. And I've watched the penalties for DUI get worse and worse over the years. Rather than be another cog in the state's DUI factory, which takes in so many good people and churns out so many convicted criminals, I decided that it would be better to be a wrench in that system.

I would rather help good people get out of a bad situation than put them in jail and burden them with massive fines and a criminal record that will only serve as an obstacle to establishing a productive life. That is why I wrote this book. Over the years, I have been fortunate to help hundreds of people with their DUI charges, and I've had a lot of success in doing so. Getting a case dismissed or hearing the words "not guilty" from a jury has been much more rewarding than obtaining convictions ever was.

My hope is that the book will serve as an educational resource that will shed some light on DUI laws and the criminal justice system. Whether or not you end up hiring a lawyer to represent you in your DUI case, it is important to educate yourself so that you have a better understanding of your situation.

If you have additional questions after reading this book, I am happy to answer them. I try to make myself as available as possible to talk to people facing criminal charges.

Nathan D. Leonardo

CONTENTS

CHAPTER 1

HOW POLICE DECIDE WHO TO STOP AND INVESTIGATE FOR DUI

So you had a couple of drinks with dinner and you're driving down the road, trying to be especially cautious to drive carefully so as not to draw the attention of the police. You don't really feel like you're impaired by the alcohol or over the legal limit, but there's no way to tell for sure, and you could do without the hassle of a police investigation. You wonder what the police are looking for, aside from the fact that you just left a restaurant or bar late at night.

Police officers are actually trained to look for specific things when searching for drunk drivers at night. Their training is based on information provided by the National Highway Traffic Safety Administration (NHTSA), which has done studies on this type of thing. According to NHTSA, certain driving behaviors are supposed to be cues or clues of impaired driving.

The reality is that a DUI officer, particularly late at night, is looking for any reason to pull you over. These are called "pretextual stops" because the officer doesn't really care about the violation but really just wants to check to see if you're DUI. He or she is just using the violation as a pretext, or excuse, to pull you over. In Arizona, pretext stops are legal. Be aware that any kind of traffic or equipment violation, no matter how trivial, is justification enough for the police to stop you. So if you have a headlight or license plate light that's not working, a cracked windshield, or even window tint that is too dark, you are essentially giving the police the ability to stop you at any time. So make sure your vehicle is well maintained. Once they have you pulled over, they are looking for any signs or symptoms of intoxication that can justify a DUI investigation.

Even though pretext stops are legal, they can be distasteful to a jury. I have had cases where the jury found my client not guilty simply because it did not believe the officers had a valid reason to make a traffic stop. Anytime a jury believes an officer is not being truthful or is abusing his or her power, you have a chance of winning at trial.

The list of driving cues provided by NHTSA is actually pretty long. It contains twenty-four different driving behaviors. NHTSA claims that if an officer sees any of these cues, there's a certain probability that the driver may be over the legal limit. The probability increases when an officer sees more than one driving cue.

Some of the cues are surprising. For instance, speeding is not a driving cue, but driving slower than the speed limit is. Of course, you'll still get pulled over for speeding, but at least it's hard for a prosecutor to argue at trial that speeding is evidence of impairment by alcohol or drugs. A lot of people who have had something to drink may be excessively careful and, as a result, drive too slowly. Of course, many people who notice that a police officer is following them will also drive too slowly. This is the problem; there are often other reasons for these driving cues, but a DUI officer will almost always interpret your driving as evidence of impairment.

Some of the driving cues are things that most drivers do out of habit. The "wide right turn," for example, is one of the most common reasons I see for a traffic stop. This is a traffic violation that occurs when you make a right turn, and you don't completely stay within the lane closest to the curb. In other words, some part of your vehicle goes over the lane divider line as you make the turn. According to NHTSA, this is also a driving cue that indicates impairment. The reason I hate to see people being stopped for this is because it's extremely common. Based on my own observations while driving around Tucson, people make wide right turns more often than not. This is especially true when they are driving pickups or SUVs with a wider turning radius. Of course, many people are simply lazy, not paying attention, or have no idea that this is illegal.

I'm not the only one who's seen this. I know another attorney who, in an effort to challenge one of these stops, sent an investigator out to the intersection where his client allegedly made a wide right turn. The investigator sat there for an hour and kept track of all the people making right turns. Although I forget the exact statistics, the number of people who made wide right turns was well over 50 percent. He then tried to argue that a wide right turn was not enough to establish reasonable suspicion for the traffic stop based on this logic: if wide right turns are the norm, then they can't be considered "suspicious." Unfortunately, this argument was not successful.

Several of the NHTSA driving cues are not traffic violations. While the police can stop you if they see you commit any legitimate traffic violation, a driving cue that is not a violation does not always justify a traffic stop. A couple of common driving cues in DUI cases are "weaving within the lane" and "weaving across lane lines." These aren't necessarily traffic violations, so a police officer would probably need to see more than this to make a stop. In fact, there is case law in Arizona that says a momentary deviation from your lane isn't enough to justify a traffic stop. I've had several cases dismissed for this reason. Additionally, if a police officer stops you because he mistakenly thinks that you have committed a traffic violation when you actually have not, the stop is not justified.

NHTSA Driving Cues

Here is the complete list of NHTSA driving cues:

- weaving
- weaving across lane lines
- straddling a lane line
- swerving
- turning with wide radius
- drifting
- almost striking object or vehicle
- stopping problems
- accelerating or decelerating rapidly
- varying speed
- slow speed (10 mph plus under limit)
- driving in opposing lanes or wrong way on one-way street
- slow response to traffic signals
- slow or failure to respond to officer's signals
- stopping in lane for no apparent reason
- driving without headlights at night
- failure to signal or signal inconsistent with action
- following too closely
- improper or unsafe lane change
- illegal or improper turn (too fast, jerky, sharp, etc.)
- driving on other than designated roadway
- stopping inappropriately in response to officer
- inappropriate or unusual behavior (throwing objects, arguing, etc.)
- appearing to be impaired

Some of these things are pretty obvious, while others are pretty innocuous. Some of these things are also somewhat subjective. Of course, the officer's reason for making a traffic stop can be challenged in court. I've had numerous cases dismissed because the stop was based only on a single, momentary crossing of a lane line, for example, or on driving behavior that the officer mistakenly thought was a traffic violation.

Even when there is no traffic stop, a police detention can sometimes be successfully challenged. For example, one of my clients, Stephen, was sleeping in his car, in the driveway of his own home, when the police pulled up behind him and blocked him in. He and his roommate, who was been the designated driver that night, had returned home from a concert. Stephen was asleep when they arrived home, so his roommate left him in the car to sleep because he didn't want to wake him. Despite this explanation, the police arrested Stephen for DUI. He was flabbergasted. The judge dismissed the case because the police had detained Stephen, by blocking him from moving his car, without any reasonable suspicion that a crime had occurred.

Post-Stop Cues/Signs and Symptoms

Once a driver has been pulled over, the police are trained to look for signs and symptoms of impairment to justify a DUI investigation. NHTSA also provides a list of "post-stop cues." These include:

- difficulty with motor vehicle controls
- difficulty exiting the vehicle
- fumbling with driver's license or registration
- repeating questions or comments
- swaying, unsteady, or balance problems
- leaning on the vehicle or other object
- slurred speech, slow to respond to officer/officer must repeat
- providing incorrect information, changes to answers
- odor of alcoholic beverage from the driver

The "signs and symptoms" I read about in almost every police report are: red, watery, bloodshot eyes; odor of alcohol; flushed or pale face; and slow, slurred, or "thick-tongued" speech. The similarity among police reports in this respect is uncanny. Sometimes I think these officers just copy and paste from their old reports.

There are some things you can do to prepare yourself for this situation. First, be organized. Have your license in a place that is easily accessible. Keep your glove compartment clean and have your registration and proof of insurance together in a small, clear plastic folder or document holder. Then you can simply hand this to the officer without even trying to take each individual document out. Second, be wary of what the officer is looking for. Be careful getting out of your car, and don't lean on the car. Don't ask him questions or ask him to repeat himself, and keep your talking to a minimum.

A lot of these signs and symptoms can be explained by things other than impairment by alcohol or drugs. For instance, most people do have red or bloodshot eyes when it's late at night and they're tired. Many people will have a flushed face when they are embarrassed by being pulled over and investigated, or made to perform coordination tests in public. And the odor of alcohol is basically meaningless because it doesn't tell the officer how much you've had to drink. It may be evidence of drinking, but it's not illegal to drink and then drive. It's only illegal to drink to the point where you are either impaired or reach a 0.08 BAC and then drive, so the odor of alcohol is not evidence of impairment.

Your explanations for these signs and symptoms may be legitimate, but there's no point in having this conversation with a police officer. No matter what you say, the officer will interpret these things as signs and symptoms of impairment. That's how he or she was trained, and you will not get the benefit of the doubt. However, you can take some comfort in the fact that, when the case goes to court, the law says that you should get the benefit of the doubt and that you are presumed innocent until proven guilty.

CHAPTER 2

MISDEMEANOR DUI VERSUS FELONY DUI

When people hear that they have been charged with "extreme DUI" or "super-extreme DUI," they often jump to the conclusion that they are facing felony DUI charges. After all, what kind of DUI can be worse than a super-extreme DUI?

The truth is that these are just scary names for different types of misdemeanor DUIs. An extreme DUI is charged when you have a blood or breath alcohol content (BAC) of 0.150 or greater. A super-extreme DUI is charged when you have a BAC of 0.200 or greater. In fact, an extreme or super-extreme DUI is a class one misdemeanor in Arizona, just like a regular DUI.

The maximum penalties for all misdemeanor DUIs in Arizona are the same, but the minimum sentence increases for an extreme DUI and increases further for a super-extreme DUI. In misdemeanor DUI cases, it is the minimum sentences that are most important because judges generally tend to impose them, unless there is something particularly aggravating about the facts of the case. (For more on these penalties, check out chapter 15.)

So what's the difference between a misdemeanor and a felony? Technically, it has to do with the maximum amount of time you're facing if convicted. It also determines what type of time you're facing. The maximum term of incarceration for a misdemeanor in Arizona is six months. The maximum term of incarceration for a felony is over one year. But the type of incarceration is also different. If you are convicted of a misdemeanor, the judge can impose a jail sentence but not a prison sentence. If you're convicted of a felony, you can go to prison.

There is a big difference between jail and prison. For instance, work release is often available while serving a jail sentence but is not available while serving a prison sentence. A felony conviction will also result in the loss of your civil rights (right to vote, serve as a juror, and bear arms) and will usually have more severe collateral consequences (like negative impact on employment, immigration status…). So, while a misdemeanor DUI conviction can carry some pretty severe penalties, it is far better than being a convicted felon.

Felony DUI

Although the majority of DUI cases are misdemeanors, there are also felony DUIs. In Arizona, they are called aggravated DUIs. There are basically four ways you can be charged with an aggravated DUI in Arizona:

1. This is your third DUI conviction within the last seven years.
2. The DUI occurred while your driver's license was suspended, cancelled or revoked because of a prior DUI or because of certain other vehicular crimes.
3. A child under fifteen years old was a passenger in the car while you were DUI.
4. The DUI occurred while you were ordered by the court to equip your vehicle with an ignition interlock device.

Most aggravated DUI convictions carry a mandatory prison sentence, which is typically followed by a term of probation with special aggravated DUI terms. If you end up causing an accident that injures or kills another person, you can also be charged with felony aggravated assault. This is usually charged as a dangerous nature offense, for which Arizona law mandates a five- to fifteen-year prison sentence. If someone is killed in the accident, you can be charged with murder.

All the defenses for a misdemeanor DUI can also be applied to felony DUI charges, but sometimes additional defenses are available. I had one case, for example, in which the Motor Vehicle Division (MVD) sent my client, Fred, a series of confusing and contradictory letters about the status of his license. Although Fred had several prior DUI convictions, the jury thought these letters were so confusing that they decided he did not have notice that his license was suspended. As a result, they found Fred not guilty of the aggravated DUI charges and guilty only of misdemeanor DUI. After getting a time-served sentence (ten days in jail), Fred was glad that he had rejected the prosecutor's initial plea offer that had required a ten-year prison sentence!

There are other defenses in aggravated assault cases as well. The state must prove that the accident was caused by the defendant's impaired driving. Another client, Jimmy, was driving home from a long day volunteering at an air show at the Air Force base. He had been drinking some beer but was more tired than impaired by alcohol. A motorcyclist swerved in front of him and stopped quickly as he was slowing down for a red light. Jimmy couldn't stop his large SUV quickly enough and bumped into the motorcycle, which fell over to the side. The motorcyclist suffered a fractured wrist, and Jimmy was charged with aggravated assault and DUI. Jimmy was very sorry that the motorcyclist was injured, but five to ten years in prison for aggravated assault didn't seem fair.

Even though Jimmy was an elderly man and a decorated veteran, the prosecutor insisted that he serve a prison sentence. With great trepidation, he declined the prison-only plea offer, knowing that he was risking several years of his life. The jury ultimately found him not guilty because they decided that his impairment didn't cause the accident. They even found him not guilty of misdemeanor DUI. It didn't hurt that the alleged victim, who had already received a large settlement from Jimmy's insurance company, was asking for tens of thousands of dollars more in criminal restitution. It just goes to show that you never know what will happen at trial.

CHAPTER 3

CHARGED WITH MORE THAN ONE DUI?

A lot of people wonder how they can be charged with multiple counts of DUI based on a single incident. The misdemeanor DUI statute contains several paragraphs, each of which sets forth a separate crime with different elements. The first paragraph prohibits driving or being in actual physical control of a vehicle while "impaired to the slightest degree." This paragraph doesn't require a chemical test or a specific blood or breath alcohol concentration (BAC). The second paragraph prohibits having a BAC over 0.08 within two hours of driving or being in actual physical control of a vehicle, the third prohibits a BAC over 0.15, and so forth. So it's actually more common to be charged with multiple counts of DUI than to only be charged with one count.

When the police decide to take a sample of your blood rather than administering a breath test, they will not immediately know your BAC. In these cases they will initially charge you under the first paragraph of the DUI statute and then later, when the crime lab has completed its analysis, the state will add any additional DUI charges based on results: if the result is over a 0.08 they will add a DUI charge under the second paragraph of the DUI statute; if the result is over 0.15, they will add an extreme DUI charge; if it's over a 0.20, they will add the super-extreme DUI charge; and if the results show the presence of illegal drugs or their metabolites, they will add a drug DUI charge.

Because each of these DUI charges is a distinct offense that has different elements the state is required to prove, multiple DUIs arising out of the same incident do not violate double jeopardy. Because each DUI charge requires proof of different elements, the type of DUI charges you're facing can affect what evidence is presented at trial and what kind of arguments you can make to the jury. Fortunately, even though all these DUI charges are technically separate crimes under Arizona law, you will not be facing separate penalties for each one. The sentences for different DUI charges based on the same incident normally all run at the same time and can't be stacked on top of each other. Misdemeanor DUIs in Arizona all have the same maximum penalty, but the minimum penalties and the consequences to your driver's license do vary depending on the charge.

One unfortunate aspect of being charged with multiple counts of DUI is that it presents the jury with the opportunity to compromise. If they can't unanimously decide on a guilty or not guilty verdict, the jury may just "split the baby" and find a defendant guilty of one charge but not the other. They usually don't realize that it really doesn't makes much difference whether there is one DUI conviction or two; the penalty will often be the same.

CHAPTER 4

FIELD SOBRIETY TESTS: ARE THEY REQUIRED?

What are field sobriety tests? These are the coordination tests that police officers administer on the side of the road. They are usually the second most critical portion of a DUI investigation, behind the testing of blood or breath. The tests are "standardized," meaning they are supposed to be done the same way, under similar conditions, every time. Some of them are also "validated," meaning they are supposedly supported by scientific studies. There are also some field sobriety tests that aren't validated but are still sometimes used by the police.

There are a couple ways to challenge field sobriety tests. First, because they are standardized and must be done the same way every time, they must be done the right way to have any value as evidence. If the officer deviates from the way the NHTSA says the tests are supposed to be done, then the test is invalid. Second, the tests are not applicable in certain situations. If someone is elderly, obese, or has certain injuries or medical conditions, the tests may not be valid.

HGN Test (Eye Test)

The validated tests include the Horizontal Gaze Nystagmus test (HGN), the Walk-and-Turn test, and the One-Leg Stand test. The HGN test is an eye test where the officer asks you to follow a stimulus (usually penlight or sometimes simply his or her finger) with your eyes as the stimulus moves back and forth. The officer is looking for an involuntary jerking of the eyeball called a nystagmus. We all have nystagmus all the time because the movement of our eyes is controlled by small muscles that simply do not operate in a completely smooth manner. The nystagmus is slowed down to the point that it's visible to the naked eye when someone has consumed alcohol.

Of course, there are many other things besides alcohol that can cause nystagmus to be visible to the naked eye. In fact, NHTSA's own studies reveal that HGN can be caused by much lower levels of alcohol than the legal limit. Nonetheless, this is supposed to be the most "scientific" of the standardized field sobriety tests and is claimed by NHTSA to be the most accurate in predicting that someone's BAC is over the legal limit.

A police officer has to be properly certified to administer this test for the results to be admissible. A certified officer must also keep a log of his or her HGN tests and the state should disclose these logs in a DUI case. Sometimes the logs reveal that an officer, although certified, has not been very accurate recently or is not particularly accurate in a certain type of DUI case.

Walk-and-Turn Test and One-Leg Stand Test

The other two most commonly used tests are the Walk-and-Turn test and the One-Leg Stand test. The NHTSA manual warns that these tests may not be valid for the elderly, people who are overweight, people who have injuries that might affect their balance, or people who are wearing high heels.

The Walk-and-Turn test requires you to take nine heel-to-toe steps in a straight line, turn, and then take nine heel-to-toe steps back. The NHTSA manual requires that police use a designated straight line, but it's not uncommon to see officers use an imaginary line. This ends up making the test subjective, since no one really knows where the line is, and virtually meaningless as evidence.

During this test the officer is obviously looking for problems with balance and whether you step off the line, but also some less obvious things like: whether you stay "in position" while he or she gives the instructions; whether he or she has to repeat the instructions; whether your heel is within one-half inch of your toe on each step; whether you turn taking a series of small steps, as instructed, or simply pivot; whether you raise your arms from your sides for balance; and whether you take the wrong number of steps.

For the One-Leg Stand test, you have to stand on one foot with the other raised at least six inches off the ground, with the toe point-ed, for thirty seconds. Meanwhile, you must look down at your foot and keep your arms at your sides. Even if you can get through the thirty seconds without dropping your foot, the officer will be look-ing to see if you are swaying, if you hop, or if you use your arms for balance.

These tests are both basically coordination tests, but there are so many little things the police are looking for that you can easily fail these tests, even if you are perfectly coordinated. They always claim that these tests also test your ability to do "divided attention" tasks like driving, which allows them to equate poor performance on the tests with im-paired driving.

As you can see, these tests are pretty subjective, despite the fact that they are "standardized." So, even though you may feel like you feel like you did well, the police will probably have a different view. It is very rare to see a police report where someone has actually "passed" the field sobriety tests. It's important to remember that, according to NHTSA, these tests are not valid for the elderly, the obese, or people with leg, foot, ankle, or other injuries that affect their balance.

Are They Required?

Do you have to take these tests if a police officer asks you to? The short answer is no. You don't have to take these tests, and there's really not a lot of downside to refusing to do them. The prosecutor can use your refusal to take the tests as evidence against you at trial, but that's usually better than having the prosecutor go through every little thing you allegedly did wrong on the tests as evidence of your impairment. The tests provide the prosecutor with a lot of ammunition to use against you. Without them, there's usually not a lot of evidence for them to present to the jury in a DUI case.

Sure, they'll argue that you refused to do the test because you knew you would fail, so you must be guilty, but the truth is that there are many good reasons to refuse to take the tests. You might have an injury or medical condition that could affect your performance. You might be a generally uncoordinated person or have bad balance. You might be too tired or nervous to comfortably perform the tests. You might think that bad weather or the physical condition of the test location would make the tests unfair. You might not trust the police officer to accurately and objectively record your performance. All of these reasons can be explained to a jury.

Of course, refusing to take the tests is a lot easier said than done. A lot of people end up taking these tests just because they find it very difficult to say no to a police officer. There's a lot of pressure to comply, and the police sometimes even threaten arrest when confronted with a refusal. Police in Arizona do have the discretion in DUI cases to either take you to jail or cite and release you, so that makes refusal even scarier. But it takes a lot of time for the police to take you to jail and book you, and in most cases they will try to avoid it because it is inconvenient. So, as long as you are polite and otherwise cooperative, chances are that you will be cited and released for a misdemeanor DUI, even if you refuse to take field sobriety tests.

Many people are also tempted to take the tests because they feel like they can pass them and that they can prove they are not intoxicated. But there's not a lot of upside to this. Not only is passing these tests rare for the reasons discussed, but I have seen a number of cases where a person has passed one or two field sobriety tests and is still charged with DUI. By the time the police end up doing the DUI "investigation," they have often made up their minds. They've usually already pulled you over for some sort of driving behavior, smelled an "odor of alcohol," and have asked you to step out of your car to do the tests. The whole point of these tests to gather evidence against you and to make the case in court later on down the road. The tests are also used to justify additional investigation, such as searching your body through a blood or breath test.

There's really no point giving them the opportunity to create this evidence against you. The fact that a jury may hear about your refusal to take the tests later on is not, at least in my mind, a big deal. That's why I typically advise people not to take tests. If you don't have any injuries or medical conditions to use as an excuse, you can simply tell the officer that you've been advised by an attorney not to take the tests.

CHAPTER 5

BLOOD OR BREATH: CAN I CHOOSE WHICH TEST TO TAKE?

The most critical part of a DUI investigation is the chemical test. In Arizona, police will usually use a blood or breath test. You do not get to choose which type of test you take; that's up to the police. Certain agencies typically use breath tests, while others use blood tests. In the Tucson area, TPD will typically use breath tests, while the Pima County Sheriff's Department will usually draw blood. However, an agency may choose to use a different type of test depending on the circumstances. Sometimes there is a problem with the breath machine or one is not available, so TPD will have to use a blood test. Sometimes the sheriff's deputies will have a problem taking blood and will call for an Intoxilyzer 8000, which is the machine currently used for breath testing in Arizona. So whether it's a breath test or blood test is really up to the officers at the scene.

Although you don't have to agree to take a breath or blood test, there are good reasons to do so. In most cases you probably should. If you refuse to take a chemical test at the police officer's request, it triggers a one-year suspension of your driver's license. This is what's called an "implied consent suspension." When you sign up for driver's license in Arizona, you agree that you will take a chemical test anytime the officer believes that you are driving while impaired. This really isn't spelled out explicitly in the application for a driver's license, so your consent to take these tests is "implied." It doesn't make a whole lot of sense, but that's the way it is.

The other reason you should just take the test, aside from the license suspension triggered by a refusal, is that it is very easy for the officer to get a warrant to take your blood anyway. In Tucson, it takes about five minutes to make a telephone call to the judge (there's a judge on duty twenty-four hours a day) and get a warrant. Of course, the police still need to provide the judge with probable cause to get the warrant. The telephone call should be recorded, and the warrant can be challenged later in court. Once they have the warrant, however, the police can forcibly take your blood. So the police will usually be able to get a sample of your blood one way or the other, but when they have to get a warrant because you initially refuse to consent to the test, your license will likely be suspended for a year.

CHAPTER 6

EXERCISING YOUR RIGHT TO REMAIN SILENT

The right to remain silent is one of the most important constitutional rights we have, at least in terms of criminal law. When approached by the police, as a result of a traffic stop or otherwise, you don't have to speak with them or answer their questions. You can simply tell them that you do not want to talk to them. At the time of this writing, the law requires you to affirmatively tell the police you are invoking your right to remain silent if you are not in custody. Otherwise, your silence in the face of questioning can be used as evidence against you in court!

Asserting your right to remain silent is easier said than done. I can't tell you how many cases I have seen where people have basically shot themselves in the foot and made it much more difficult to defend their case because they made incriminating statements to police officers. When you're actually in that situation, with somebody in a position of authority asking you questions and even demanding answers, it's difficult to refuse to answer.

You have to remember that police officers arrest people all the time. They deal with lots of people every day who invoke their rights, and it's not something they will automatically get upset about. They may act like they're upset, but this is part of their job and they understand that people have the right to remain silent. That said, the police will want to get you to talk because they know you will probably provide them with additional evidence. You may say something incriminating and, even if you don't, they could say that your speech was slow or slurred, that you seemed confused or disoriented, or that they smelled the odor of alcohol on your breath. All these details will be presented in their reports as evidence of your impairment.

I typically tell people to politely inform the officer that you would like to invoke your right to remain silent or, if it's more comfortable, that your attorney advised you not to answer questions. It's important to be polite and otherwise cooperative. Some people think that the police officer is being so nice that they might not be charged as long as they do everything that the officer asks of them. Other people think they can just talk their way out of being charged. Remember, no matter how friendly the officers seem, or how much you think you might be able to talk yourself out of the situation, that's not what's going to happen.

The police aren't going to give you the benefit of the doubt because that's not what they're trained to do. They are trained to gather evidence against you and charge you. Nothing you say is going to change that.

Just about all the questions that the police ask, even from their first contact with you, are designed to gather evidence. If they pull you over, they may initially ask if you know why you were stopped. If you say "yes, I committed such-and-such violation," you can rest assured that this will be in the police report and will be used to corroborate their claim that they had reasonable suspicion to make the stop. They may follow up by asking whether you've had anything to drink. If you say I only had a couple beers, then that justifies a continued detention and DUI investigation. If you say no, and a blood or breath test later shows alcohol in your system, then you will be portrayed in court as a liar. This could really damage your credibility, whether you choose to testify or not.

If you let them, the police will usually go on to ask you a bunch of questions listed on the DUI forms they normally use. These include trick questions, like: "on a scale of one to ten, with one being completely sober and ten being falling down drunk, where would you place yourself?" If you circle any number besides one, then this will be presented in court as a confession or admission to being "impaired to the slightest degree," which means you're guilty of DUI.

As you can see, answering any of these questions puts yourself in a no-win situation. It's better to say nothing at all than to say something that can be used against you. Just do yourself a favor: don't engage in a conversation with the police, and don't answer their questions.

CHAPTER 7

MIRANDA RIGHTS: EVERYTHING YOU NEED TO KNOW

One of the most common questions I get as a criminal defense attorney is "what if the police didn't read me my Miranda rights?" Many people are under the mistaken impression that if the police didn't read them their rights, then their charges will be dismissed. That's not the way it works. A police officer is free to ask you questions, and you are free to assert your right to remain silent at any time. Under *Miranda v. Arizona*, a police officer is only required to read you your rights prior to "custodial interrogation." This means that two things must happen: (1) you must be in custody, and (2) you must be interrogated.

You are in custody for purposes of *Miranda* if, based on the totality of the circumstances, your freedom of movement has been restrained in a significant way and you are aware of this restraint. This usually means you are arrested, but courts can look at a variety of factors in making this determination. These include the location of the questioning, the duration of the questioning, statements made during the questioning, and the use of restraints. Thus, depending on the facts of your case, a criminal defense attorney may be able to argue that you were "in custody" before you were formally arrested.

You are being interrogated for purposes of *Miranda* if the police are questioning you and their questions are designed or likely to elicit an incriminating response. Although most questions the police ask are designed to gather information that they can use as evidence against you, the government may argue that some of their questions were not.

The Miranda Rights

1. You have the right to remain silent.
2. Anything you say can and will be used against you in a court of law.
3. You have the right to talk to a lawyer and have him present with you while you are being questioned.
4. If you cannot afford to hire a lawyer, one will be appointed to represent you before any questioning if you wish.
5. You can decide at any time to exercise these rights and not answer any questions or make any statements.

So what happens if the police don't read you your rights under these circumstances? The case doesn't get dismissed, but any statements you made should be suppressed. In other words, the statements cannot be used as evidence against you in court. Obviously, this only helps you if you made an incriminating statement in the first place. But, if you made the mistake of talking to the police and they didn't read you your rights when they should have, suppression of your statements may be very helpful. While this can certainly increase your odds of a successful defense, the government will still probably have enough additional evidence to continue prosecuting the case. In addition, even if your statements are suppressed, they can still be used to cross-examine you if you choose to testify and your testimony is inconsistent with the suppressed statements.

It is wise to invoke both your right to remain silent and your right to an attorney when being questioned by the police. If you simply invoke your right to remain silent without requesting an attorney, the police can actually continue in their attempts to question you. Once you ask for an attorney, the police must stop questioning you until you have an attorney. Not only do you have the right to consult with an attorney, but you have the right to have an attorney present during questioning.

Of course, the police will not have an attorney on call to represent you, so your invocation of this right should end all interrogation for the remainder of your interaction with them. They may give you a chance to try to call an attorney for a consultation, but chances are you will not actually get an attorney to represent you until shortly before you go to court. If you do get ahold of a lawyer, they will likely advise you to invoke your right to remain silent and have an attorney present.

CHAPTER 8

HOW CAN I GET A DUI IF I WASN'T EVEN DRINKING?

Illegal Drugs

We always hear about the problem of drinking and driving, but the truth is that neither drinking nor driving is actually required to be convicted of a DUI. There are a couple of ways to be charged with DUI when you haven't been drinking. First, you can be charged with DUI for driving after having consumed any illegal drug (marijuana, cocaine, methamphetamine, heroine…). If any of these drugs, or even their metabolites (the substances that present after the body has metabolized the drug itself) are present in your body while driving, you can be charged with a drug DUI. Impairment is not required.

This is especially problematic for drugs like marijuana, which can stay in your system for an extended period of time. There are ways to get around certain marijuana DUIs—the courts have determined that a certain metabolite of marijuana doesn't count because it's not psychoactive, and there are some additional defenses available to people with medical marijuana cards, which is a whole other subject—but these things will not stop you from being charged in the first place.

If the police suspect drug use, they will often conduct what's called a drug recognition examination (DRE), in addition to the normal DUI investigation. The exam is an attempt to identify what type of drug is affecting you and can only be administered by officers who are certified to do it. The exam includes things like checking a person's pulse, temperature, pupils, muscle tone, and sense of time. The police will usually assume drug use when they think they've seen impairment, but a breath test shows no alcohol. However, they may not have probable cause for a blood test or DUI arrest unless they conduct a DRE. This is another reason that it's generally best not to answer their questions.

Medications and Prescription Drugs

The second way to be charged with a DUI, even though you haven't been drinking, is by having taken medication. Of course, the only way the police would know about your medication is if you told them you're taking it, or they saw a prescription bottle. Even so, these cases are not uncommon.

Having a prescription for a medication can be a defense to a drug DUI, assuming you are using the medication appropriately as prescribed, but it is not a defense to an "impaired-to-the-slightest-degree DUI." Certain medications, particularly opiates, can cause impairment. In fact, many come with warnings against driving while using the medication. Even if you are using your medications properly, you will still be charged with a DUI if the police think you are impaired.

A lot of the prescription medication cases involve issues about how much medication was taken and whether the amount in someone's blood is within the therapeutic range. Some of these are more difficult for the state to prove because the criminalists who test the blood are not doctors and are typically not well trained with regard to all these different medications and their effects on the human body. It may also be hard for them to testify that the amount of a particular medication in the blood was higher than the therapeutic range for a person with a particular medical problem, because that often depends on how long a person has taken the medication and what kind of tolerance has been developed.

Because people are taking medication to combat some kind of mental or physical problem, it can sometimes be argued that the medication is actually making them a better driver and alleviating the mental or physical problem that actually does impair the person. This was the case with my client Katie, a registered nurse, who had been taking prescribed antianxiety and antidepressant medications after losing her husband and two children in successive freak accidents over a very short period of time. Katie was so distraught and depressed that she couldn't even appear for her own trial. She probably shouldn't have been driving in the first place, but the state had a hard time proving that her bad driving was due to the medication rather than the mental impairment that the medication was intended to alleviate. The jury thought there was a reasonable doubt about this and found Katie not guilty.

Although having a prescription and using this medication in accordance with the prescription is a defense to the drug DUI statute, it's difficult to get doctors to testify. As a result, the defendant may be forced to testify in order to present the required evidence concerning his or her prescription. Keep in mind, though, that the state may still argue that you were impaired by the medication, even if you can prove that it was prescribed. They will do this using the typical evidence gathered during the DUI investigation—bad driving, field sobriety tests, statements, behavior, and other observations—and evidence gathered through a DRE, if one was done.

CHAPTER 9

HOW CAN I GET A DUI IF I WASN'T EVEN DRIVING?

When people think of DUI, they usually imagine someone weaving down the road or otherwise driving erratically. In Arizona, that's not always the case. In fact, you don't even have to drive at all to be charged with DUI. The charge of driving under the influence in Arizona requires that a person is either driving a vehicle or is in *actual physical control* of a vehicle.

Now there are occasionally cases in which someone is charged with DUI even though they were neither driving nor in actual physical control, but those are fairly rare. Sometimes it is difficult to determine who was driving a vehicle. For example, when police are called to the scene of a reported accident, especially when it is a single-car accident and there are multiple people who were in the vehicle, it can sometimes be difficult to determine who was driving. They may mistakenly believe you were driving, even though you weren't. However, these situations usually provide the defense with a lot of reasonable doubt to work with at trial.

The more common way to be charged with DUI when you aren't driving is to be in actual physical control of a vehicle. DUI charges under the "actual physical control" theory are fairly common. Many times police will find someone drunk inside of a vehicle—sometimes even passed out or sleeping behind the wheel—and decide to charge the person with DUI because they determine that he or she was in actual physical control of the vehicle.

Actual Physical Control Factors

Simply being drunk inside a vehicle, even when you're not sitting in the driver's seat, may be enough to prove a DUI charge. There are a number of factors that the law says should be considered in deciding whether someone is in actual physical control:

- whether the vehicle was running or the ignition was on
- where the keys are located
- where and in what position the person was found in the vehicle
- whether the person was awake or asleep
- whether the vehicle's lights were on
- whether the vehicle was stopped or parked and where
- whether the driver had voluntarily pulled off the road
- the time of day and the weather conditions
- whether the heater or air conditioner was on
- whether the windows were up or down
- any explanation of the circumstances shown by the evidence

This is not an all-inclusive list, so other factors may also be considered.

The people who weigh these factors are usually jurors, since whether someone is in actual physical control is a highly factual determination. Ultimately, jurors should be instructed that someone is not in actual physical control unless they actually posed a threat to the public by the exercise of present or imminent control of the vehicle while impaired. It's not your subjective intent that matters, only the objective facts.

How does this play out at trial? A few years ago I had a DUI client, Chad, who was also an attorney and was very concerned about the ramifications a DUI conviction would have on his license. He had dropped off his car at a gas station and then went out drinking with a friend. Afterwards, his friend brought him back to his car at the gas station. Chad had probably had too much to drink and was tired, so he called another friend to pick him up and take him home. While he was waiting, he fell asleep in the driver's seat of his car. Someone from the gas station saw him and called the police, who came and arrested Chad for DUI. The friend never showed up but was willing to testify at trial that Chad had called him for a ride. The jury found Chad not guilty because he was simply using his car as a temporary shelter and was not in actual physical control. He didn't intend to drive and was actually trying to do the right thing.

If you've been drinking, it's better to sleep in your car than to drive it; but if you want to make sure that you're not charged with DUI, you probably shouldn't sleep in your car either. If you have to sleep in your car, then remember the actual physical control factors and think about how a judge or jury might interpret the circumstances. Obviously, it would behoove you to lie down in the back seat, make sure the engine and lights are off, and put the keys somewhere that is difficult to access.

CHAPTER 10

CAN I BE CONVICTED OF DUI IF I AM UNDER THE LEGAL LIMIT?

The DUI laws in Arizona make it illegal to drive while "impaired to the slightest degree" by alcohol, drugs, or any combination of the two. This language doesn't require a chemical test at all, much less a certain breath or blood alcohol concentration. You can be charged if the police simply believe you are impaired by alcohol, based on their observations and your performance on the field sobriety tests.

That said, it is very rare to see a DUI case where there was no chemical test. Even if there were substantial evidence of impairment, it would be difficult for the state, without a chemical test, to prove beyond a reasonable doubt that the impairment was due to alcohol or drugs. But what if a breath or blood test is done and the results are below the legal limit? The simple answer is that you can still be prosecuted for DUI if the state believes you were impaired. It ultimately comes down to "prosecutorial discretion."

The "legal limit" for a basic DUI in Arizona has changed a couple of times over the years—and it always gets lower. Most recently, the limit for a basic misdemeanor DUI was reduced from 0.10 to 0.08. There are special interest groups lobbying for an even lower limit of 0.05. Just because your BAC is below 0.08, however, doesn't mean that you're not impaired to the slightest degree.

Some of the decision whether to prosecute depends on how close to 0.08 the BAC is. Of course, the closer your BAC is to 0.08, the more likely you are to be prosecuted. In Arizona, juries are instructed that there is a legal presumption that the defendant is not under the influence if his or her BAC is below a 0.05, so that makes low BAC cases especially difficult to prosecute.

The other consideration is whether there is enough evidence of impairment, aside from the chemical test, to prove that you were impaired while driving or being in actual physical control of your vehicle. Your performance on the field sobriety tests will be a significant factor, as will your behavior and any statements or admissions you made. When I began my career as a prosecutor doing DUI cases almost twenty years ago, we would take quite a few 0.06–0.07 cases to trial. I'm not sure why—if it's budget cuts or simply more reasonable people at the helm—but this doesn't seem to happen as much anymore.

CHAPTER 11

WHAT WILL HAPPEN TO MY DRIVER'S LICENSE?

One thing that people sometimes overlook when dealing with a DUI case is the effect of the DUI charge on their driver's license. There are three types of license suspensions that can occur in an Arizona DUI case: (1) an admin-per-se suspension, (2) a suspension resulting from conviction, and (3) an implied consent suspension.

The first two types of suspensions last for at least ninety days, although you can usually get a restricted driving permit after the first thirty days. The third kind of suspension only occurs if you refuse to take a chemical test. In that case, your license will be suspended for an entire year (two years if you have a prior refusal). This is an important aspect of every DUI case because most people need to be able to drive in order to earn a living and take care of their family, especially in a state like Arizona that is so geographically spread out, with limited public transportation options.

Admin-Per-Se Suspension

In Arizona, just being charged with a DUI usually results in the MVD attempting to suspend your license. This is called an admin-per-se suspension. This type of license suspension is an administrative proceeding that is completely separate from the criminal case. So even if you win your DUI case, your license can still be suspended by the MVD. Usually, the suspension will be automatically imposed unless you request a hearing within fifteen days. If you do request a hearing, the suspension will be stayed until the hearing occurs. In other words, you can at least delay the suspension by requesting a hearing. The MVD has its own judges, called hearing officers, who determine whether a license suspension should be imposed.

A common question people have is "how can they suspend my license if I haven't been convicted?" The answer is a bit confusing, but I'll try to explain. In Arizona, driving is considered a privilege rather than a right. When the state of Arizona grants you the privilege of driving by giving you a driver's license, you implicitly agree that this driving privilege will be suspended if you are arrested for DUI and have a blood alcohol concentration (BAC) that is over the legal limit. You also implicitly agree that you will take a chemical test if you are suspected of DUI, which is why refusal to take a chemical test results in a one-year suspension. This is called the admin per se/implied consent agreement and it's basically a contract (although not written, just implied) that you have made with the state in order to enjoy the privilege of driving.

Challenging the Admin-Per-Se Suspension

Usually, when an officer charges you with a DUI and has a breath test result showing that you are over the legal limit, he or she will serve you with a notice of admin-per-se suspension at the scene. When a blood sample is taken instead of a breath test, the officer may not serve you with the notice of suspension at the scene. If they do, then you might want to request a summary review of the officer's certified report. When you ask for a summary review, a hearing officer will examine the officer's report to see if it contains enough evidence to uphold the suspension. If the summary review occurs before the blood test is completed, there is usually insufficient evidence to uphold the suspension.

If a blood sample is taken and the officer does not serve you with a notice of suspension at the scene, the notice will be mailed to you (at the address you have on record with MVD) after the crime lab tests the blood and finds the result to be over the legal limit. Whether you receive notice of the admin-per-se suspension at the scene or in the mail, the suspension will begin automatically unless you request a hearing within fifteen days of receiving the notice.

If you request a hearing, the license suspension will be stayed until the hearing occurs. It won't be imposed unless you lose the hearing. With admin-per-se suspensions, the MVD hearing is limited to the following issues:

- whether the officer had a reasonable belief that you were DUI
- whether you were placed under arrest for a DUI
- whether a chemical test showed that your BAC was over the limit
- whether the testing method used was valid and reliable

The state's burden of proof at these hearings is very low; the state must only prove these things by a preponderance of the evidence (more than 50 percent likely), which is a much lower burden than in a criminal case where the state must prove that you are guilty beyond a reasonable doubt. Moreover, the hearing officer also plays the role of the prosecutor. He or she will ask questions, move to admit evidence, and then rule on any objections the defense attorney may have to the evidence.

Needless to say, these hearings are difficult to win. They do, however, provide an opportunity to question the officers involved under oath and on the record. This can prove valuable later in your case.

Suspension Resulting from Conviction

Even if you are successful in challenging your administrative license suspension, you license will still be suspended if you are eventually convicted of DUI. When your license is suspended as a result of conviction, you will have to obtain an expensive SR-22 insurance policy in order to get your license back after the suspension. The admin-per-se suspension, on the other hand, only requires that you pay reinstatement fees to get your license back after the suspension. Fortunately, if you end up being subject to both types of license suspension, the MVD will usually only take action based on the admin-per-se suspension. Thus, in most of these cases your license will not be suspended twice, nor will you be required to purchase SR-22 insurance.

Implied Consent Suspension (Refusal)

In Arizona, when you refuse to take a chemical test at the officer's request, your license is suspended for an entire year. This is based on Arizona's implied consent law, which basically states that when you apply for a driver's license, you impliedly give your consent to the state to take your blood or breath, if and when you are suspected of DUI. You can also request a hearing to challenge an implied consent suspension, which will stop the suspension from being imposed until the hearing occurs. An MVD hearing in a refusal case is limited to the following issues:

- whether the officer had a reasonable belief that you were DUI
- whether you were placed under arrest for a DUI
- whether you refused to take a chemical test
- whether you were informed of the consequences of refusal

Sometimes the police are impatient and are quick to conclude that someone is refusing to submit to a test just because they ask a couple of questions. Sometimes the police don't inform a person that by refusing he or she will be subject to a one-year suspension. Sometimes, although it is rare, the police don't even show up to the hearing. If they don't show up, the suspension will usually be voided because no evidence will be presented at the hearing. In any event, it's usually worth challenging these suspensions because they are so lengthy.

CHAPTER 12

TIMELINE OF A DUI

The criminal justice system is a lot different in real life than it is on television. People are used to seeing entire cases resolved, from arrest to trial, in a single one-hour episode. The reality is that a DUI, and any criminal case for that matter, can take many months to resolve. If a case goes to trial, it is not uncommon for the trial to occur more than a year after the arrest.

One reason for this is that the courts, as well as many attorneys, are overwhelmed with a high volume of cases. The crime labs that test blood in DUI cases are also overwhelmed. Another reason is that there are often legal issues that need to be resolved prior to trial. There is a lot of work to be done in defending a DUI case: gathering disclosure, which must sometimes be compelled by court order; interviewing witnesses, researching and writing legal motions, and conducting evidentiary hearings. All this must be done before a case is ready for trial. This delay usually benefits the defense, although there are some cases that are best resolved as quickly as possible.

All criminal cases begin with an arraignment. In misdemeanor DUI cases, this is usually the court date written on the citation you are given by the police. At the arraignment, the court will assign a judge to your case and schedule another court date, which is called a pretrial conference or a case management conference, depending on the court.

There are typically a number of these court dates, usually scheduled every thirty days or so, while disclosure is being completed and investigation is being done. Fortunately, in misdemeanor cases, most Arizona courts will allow your attorney to waive your presence at most of these hearings so that you don't have to miss a lot of work. During this time there may be legal motions filed, which are then set for a hearing in front of the judge. If a plea agreement is reached, there may be a change of plea hearing scheduled. If not, then the case will eventually be set for trial.

Every case takes its own unique path through the court. It is important to prepare yourself mentally for the fact that it may be hanging over your head for a few months. There's no use worrying about the case while it is pending because there is little you can do to change what's happening, aside from obtaining legal counsel to obtain the best possible outcome. Just remain positive, keep in contact with your attorney, and continue living your life the way you otherwise would. Of course, you want to be very careful not to violate your conditions of release or commit any new offenses, which could make things much worse.

CHAPTER 13

DO I REALLY NEED AN ATTORNEY TO FIGHT MY DUI?

This is a personal question that everyone charged with a DUI must ask themselves. The answer may be different from person to person because a lot of it depends on how much you have to lose and, unfortunately, whether you can afford it.

If you are charged with a DUI in Arizona and qualify as indigent (your income is under a predetermined limit), the court should appoint a public defender or contract attorney for you. If you qualify for a public defender or appointed attorney, you are typically only required to pay a few hundred dollars to the government to offset the cost of the attorney. One caveat is that you are not entitled to the assistance of an attorney in MVD license suspension matters, so a public defender or appointed attorney will not represent you before the MVD.

If you are not satisfied with your appointed attorney, you can usually hire a private DUI lawyer while your case is still pending. You should to do this well before any trial date to ensure that your new attorney has adequate time to prepare your case. However, if for financial reasons you have no other option, an appointed attorney can be very beneficial. Because most of these attorneys are handling a very high volume of cases, it's a good idea to be proactive and highly involved in your case to ensure that your appointed attorney is also.

If you make a decent income and don't qualify for an appointed attorney, then you only have two choices: you can either hire an attorney or waive your right to an attorney and defend yourself. The second option is a scary proposition for most people, and I wouldn't recommend it. If you feel strongly that you are guilty, that there is no defense, and you simply want to accept whatever plea agreement the state decides to offer (assuming they offer one), then this could be the way to go. It's certainly cheaper than hiring an attorney to shepherd you through the process.

If you feel this way, I still recommend that you at least discuss the case with a DUI attorney to see if you might be missing something and get an idea whether you have any chance of a successful defense. An attorney who has handled a lot of these cases in the court where your case is being prosecuted can tell you whether you are being offered a fair deal and answer any other questions you might have. Most DUI attorneys offer a free consultation, so there's really no reason not to take this step.

It should be immediately apparent from a quick review of the Arizona DUI penalties detailed in chapter 15 that a DUI can have very serious consequences. The consequences are much more severe for second and third offenses. Many people who come to me to for advice about their DUI case have prior DUI convictions. Sometimes, when they describe the facts of their prior DUI cases, there are obvious issues that should have been litigated and challenged but weren't. Instead these people were simply encouraged to plead guilty as soon as possible. Unfortunately, it is very difficult and often impossible to address such issues after someone has already been convicted.

The legal, court-imposed consequences of a DUI conviction sometimes pale in comparison to the other negative consequences that a DUI conviction can have in your life. If you are convicted of DUI, you have a criminal record. Aside from the effect this can have on your reputation, it can cause other problems, depending on your unique situation. Some people lose their jobs as a result of a conviction. For others, a conviction can have ramifications for their immigration status or child custody arrangements.

With these potential consequences in mind, most people conclude that it makes sense to do whatever they can to defend themselves. No attorney can guarantee a particular result, but a good one can substantially increase your odds of a successful resolution. Hiring an attorney is expensive, but if you find the right one, the money is well spent. There is value in handing your problem, and much of the anxiety that accompanies it, over to someone trained to solve it.

CHAPTER 14

BEATING THE OVER-THE-LEGAL-LIMIT DUI: THE SECRETS THEY DON'T WANT YOU TO KNOW

People generally believe that when a breath or blood test shows that they are over the legal limit, there is no way to challenge the result, and the case might as well be over. They don't realize that breath and blood testing techniques can be flawed and that there are a host of potential legal challenges that can be made and which can result in DUI charges being dismissed, the state's evidence being precluded, or a not guilty verdict at trial. I'm here to tell you that DUI cases can be won and are won on a regular basis, even when a blood or breath test shows that the defendant is over the legal limit. Even in cases where a complete victory is unlikely, a partial victory (i.e., beating the most serious charge) can often be achieved.

Before addressing breath and blood tests specifically, it's important to note that, regardless of the test result, the alcohol or drug must have been consumed prior to driving. I have successfully defended several cases by asserting that alcohol was consumed after driving.

Daniel, for example, was driving through Gates Pass, a rural road through the mountains west of Tucson, on his way to a party where he was supposed to meet up with his wife. A deer walked into the roadway, and Daniel swerved to avoid hitting it. Someone saw him and called the police. Daniel's car ended up stuck in a ditch on the side of the road.

While he waited for his wife to come pick him up, he opened the cooler full of beer that he was taking to the party and started drinking in the desert. The police came and arrested him for DUI. Although they didn't notice any empty beer cans, they never search the area around the car. The jury accepted Daniel's explanation and found him not guilty. So it doesn't matter what your BAC turns out to be if you weren't drinking *before* driving.

Breath Tests

Breath testing in Arizona is done with a machine called the Intoxilyzer 8000. These machines come with an inherent margin of error of 10 percent. They must also be continuously calibrated and subject to quality assurance testing. It's critical to check these records. In one recent case, for example, I found that the machine essentially crashed and was taken out of service a couple weeks after my client's arrest. The state's quality assurance specialist testified that she wasn't sure what caused the problem but that the machine was working properly during my client's breath test. Nonetheless, the malfunction was enough to provide the jury with reasonable doubt about the test result and find my client not guilty.

Additionally, police officers must be properly certified to operate the Intoxilyzer 8000, and Arizona law requires that specific protocol be followed before test results can be used as evidence. This protocol includes a "deprivation period," a checklist, and two tests that are within 0.02 of each other (which in itself raises some serious questions about the accuracy of the results).

Even if this protocol is followed, there are things that can case inaccurate readings. For example, instable voltage (the machine is often plugged into a cigarette lighter in a police car) and radio frequency interference can cause problems with the machine. Alcohol trapped in dentures or chewing gum, or any other mouth alcohol, can falsely elevate the results. A person's hematocrit level (the number of red blood cells in proportion to the rest of the blood) can alter the results by up to 5 percent. Things like body temperature, breathing patterns, and even the time of day can skew the results. If the test is done while a person is still absorbing alcohol that they've consumed, this can also falsely elevate the results.

Even the way the machine is programmed to calculate its results can often be attacked at trial. It is programmed, for example, to calculate its results based on what the government has determined to be an average partition ratio. A partition ratio is the ratio of alcohol in the breath to alcohol in the blood. A breath test is really only attempting to estimate blood alcohol by analyzing breath. Since only the alcohol in the blood can cause impairment, the partition ratio is often a legitimate subject at trial. Of course, not everyone is average. Different people have different partition ratios, and these ratios can vary significantly. So much so, that a difference in partition ratio can cause up to a 40 percent difference in a breath test result!

Blood Tests

Blood tests are generally considered more accurate than breath tests, but they are still susceptible to attack. When I started prosecuting these cases, Arizona required that blood samples be taken by medical personnel. Now the police are allowed to take someone's blood on the side of the road as long as they took a phlebotomy class and got a certificate.

Blood samples are analyzed by a machine called the gas chromatograph. These machines have a 5 percent margin of error. The criminalists who test the samples at the crime lab need to have a margin of error of 10 percent to get their permit.

It is critical to obtain all the records and documentation the machine produces, not only from the test of your sample, but also from the other samples being tested at the same time. These include controls that are used to determine if the machine is working properly. It is also important to get documentation regarding calibration. An expert review of these records often reveals unidentified substances in the blood, which can indicate contamination.

There have also been issues with the controls used by local labs. They are purchased from other companies and come with their own margin of error. They also come with strict handling instructions, which must be followed for accurate results. I have seen some controls being used that aren't even certified for forensic use. These controls are important because they are what the criminalist uses to ensure that the machine is working properly.

There are also a number of fact-specific defenses in blood cases: police blood kits can expire or malfunction; the officer drawing the blood may not have used the proper procedures; different hematocrit levels can affect the BAC; coagulation or clotting can increase BAC; high levels of sodium in the blood may increase the BAC; if there was an insufficient volume of blood drawn, the preservatives in the tubes can artificially increase the BAC; if the tubes aren't sealed or stored correctly, fermentation could produce additional alcohol over time. It is critical to have the blood test reviewed in detail by someone who can spot any of these potential issues.

CHAPTER 15

POSSIBLE PENALTIES FOR A DUI

The penalties for a DUI in Arizona are substantial. The minimum sentences, particularly the minimum fines and surcharges, always seem to increase with every amendment to the DUI laws. This chapter will outline the current maximum and minimum penalties for different types of DUI convictions. In addition to these penalties, all DUI convictions in Arizona require a substance abuse evaluation and counseling, as well as the installation of an ignition interlock device on a vehicle that you operate.

Misdemeanor DUI

Impaired to the Slightest Degree or BAC Above 0.080 (A.R.S. § 28–1381):

First Offense

MAXIMUM: Six months in jail, a $2,500 fine, and five years' supervised probation.

MINIMUM: Ten days in jail; however, the court may suspend nine of the ten days if you complete the required alcohol and/or drug evaluation and submit to treatment. A $250 fine, plus a surcharge, and two additional $500 assessments.

LICENSE: The Arizona MVD will suspend your driver's license for a minimum of ninety days. After the first thirty days, you may be able to obtain a restricted license that allows you to travel to and from work, school, and/or treatment.

Second Offense

MAXIMUM: Six months in jail, a $2,500 fine, five years' supervised probation.

MINIMUM: Ninety days in jail; however, the court may suspend sixty of the ninety days if you complete the required alcohol and/or drug evaluation, and submit to treatment. A $500 fine, plus a surcharge, and two additional $1,250 assessments.

LICENSE: Your driver's license will be revoked for an entire year. After the first forty-five days, you may be able to obtain a restricted license that allows you to travel to and from work, school, and/or treatment, as long as an ignition interlock device is installed on a vehicle that you operate.

BAC 0.150 or More, aka "Extreme DUI" [A.R.S. § 28–1382(A)(1)]:

First Offense

MAXIMUM: A maximum of six months in jail, a $2,500 fine, five years of supervised probation.

MINIMUM: Thirty days in jail, a $250 fine, plus a surcharge, and three additional assessments of $250, $1,250, and $1,000.

LICENSE: The Arizona MVD will suspend your driver's license for a minimum of ninety days. After the first thirty days, you may be able to obtain a restricted license that allows you to travel to and from work, school, and/or treatment.

Second Offense

MAXIMUM: A maximum of six months in jail, a $2,500 fine, five years of supervised probation.

MINIMUM: One hundred twenty days in jail, $500 fine, plus a surcharge, two assessments of $1,250 each, and an additional assessment of $250.

LICENSE: Your driver's license will be revoked for an entire year. After the first forty-five days, you may be able to obtain a restricted license that allows you to travel to and from work, school, and/or treatment, as long as an ignition interlock device is installed on a vehicle that you operate.

BAC 0.200 or More, aka "Super-Extreme DUI" [A.R.S. § 28-1382(A)(2)]:

First Offense

MAXIMUM: A maximum of six months in jail, a $2,500 fine, five years of supervised probation.

MINIMUM: Forty-five days in jail, a $500 fine, plus a surcharge, two assessments of $1,000 each, and an additional assessment of $250.

LICENSE: The Arizona MVD will suspend your driver's license for a minimum of ninety days. After the first thirty days, you may be able to obtain a restricted license that allows you to travel to and from work, school, and/or treatment.

Second Offense

MAXIMUM: A maximum of six months in jail, a $2,500 fine, five years of supervised probation.

MINIMUM: One hundred eighty days in jail, $1,000 fine, plus a surcharge, two assessments of $1,250 each, and an additional assessment of $250.

LICENSE: Your driver's license will be revoked for an entire year. After the first forty-five days, you may be able to obtain a restricted license that allows you to travel to and from work, school, and/or treatment, as long as an ignition interlock device is installed on a vehicle that you operate.

Felony DUI
Aggravated DUI (DUI with a child under fifteen years old in vehicle)

This type of aggravated DUI is a class six felony. The maximum prison sentence for a class six felony depends on whether you have any prior felony convictions that qualify as "historical priors." If you have no prior convictions, the maximum sentence is two years in prison. With one prior conviction, the maximum sentence goes up to 2.75 years in prison. With two prior convictions, the maximum sentence goes up to 5.75 years in prison. You could also be sentenced to up to ten years of supervised probation. The maximum fine is $150,000.

The minimum sentence for this type of aggravated DUI is the same as the minimum sentence for the misdemeanor DUI that the offense would have been had there been no child in the vehicle. A conviction will also result in the revocation of your driver's license for one year and may result in the forfeiture of your vehicle.

Aggravated DUI (3rd DUI within seven years, or DUI while license is suspended or restricted)

This type of aggravated DUI is a class four felony. The maximum prison sentence for a class four felony depends on whether you have any prior felony convictions that qualify as "historical priors." If you have no prior convictions, the maximum sentence is 3.75 years in prison. With one prior conviction, the maximum sentence goes up to 7.5 years in prison. With two prior convictions, the maximum sentence goes up to fifteen years in prison. You could also be sentenced to up to ten years of supervised probation. The maximum fine is $150,000.

The minimum sentence for this type of aggravated DUI is four months in prison. If this is your fourth DUI within seven years, the minimum sentence is eight months in prison. A felony DUI conviction will also result in the revocation of your driver's license for three years and may result in the forfeiture of your vehicle.

EPILOGUE

I wrote this book as an educational resource for the general public. The criminal justice system exists to serve the public and should not be shrouded in mystery. DUI is one of the most common criminal charges in our country, and it affects nearly every demographic of society. Many people charged with a DUI have never been arrested or charged with a crime before. In most cases, they will never be arrested or charged with a crime again.

That is why these cases are so important to me. A single DUI charge can turn an otherwise law-abiding person into a "criminal" and alter the rest of his or her life. It is my hope that this book will serve to educate people about Arizona DUI law and the legal process involved in successfully defending themselves against DUI charges.

Despite what you see on billboards and television, these cases are not hopeless. It is important to educate yourself about the issues that may arise in a DUI case, and reading this book is a step in the right direction. It is also important to take the next step and consult with an experienced DUI defense attorney about the specific facts of your case.

WHAT OTHERS ARE SAYING

Outstanding and Dedicated Criminal Defense

After being charged with a DUI, I had little hope there would be any outcome other than a plea agreement including stiff penalties. Nathan Leonardo helped me remain calm and collected throughout the entire process and was insistent on keeping me informed with every update and detail that occurred along the way. His hard work eventually led to dismissal, as his defense scrutinized every aspect of the associated charges. Nathan is one of the most confident, patient, and professional attorneys I have met. While many attorneys will try to settle on a plea, Nathan continuously went the extra mile and insisted on finding any detail that would benefit my case. His persistent work ethic and commitment to his clients is exemplified in all aspects of interaction.

Grateful

I am a professional who found myself in the middle of a scary situation and needed help. The only thing that I have ever experienced was a speeding ticket and now I was having to prove my innocence. The whole court process was overwhelming and confusing but Nathan helped me to understand and to stay calm. His advice was always right on and in the end my case was dismissed with prejudice. I am so grateful to him and his caring demeanor.

Also, he was always available to talk or would call me back in a very timely manner. Great guy and a great attorney.

Lifesaver

I hired Mr. Leonardo to help represent me with a complicated history of multiple misdemeanors in Oro Valley. I was facing harsh penalties. Mr. Leonardo was patient with a consult and evaluated my case with serious detail. The day of my court appearance, Nathan arrived looking impeccable in his dress and mannerisms. The prosecutor proposed a year in jail and other penalties. Nathan argued my case with specifics and the Judge arrived at 48 hours of jail for my sentence. I was relieved. The Judge acknowledged that I had found a "very competent attorney." I thoroughly agree. Nathan followed up my case in a timely manner. I'm incredibly grateful for his help and will contact him if needed in the future.

Great Lawyer

I can't say enough about Mr. Leonardo! He's a very informative and knowledgeable person and he handled my case perfectly! I will now be recommending him to all friends and family if they ever need representation in any legal matter!

Excellent Lawyer

I was arrested for DUI in November 2013. My BAC was .124/.126, the legal limit is .08. I thought I was never going be able to prove my innocence, so I contemplated pleading guilty, but the penalties for a DUI is worse than the crime itself. Nathan Leonardo was recommended to me by another attorney. I am VERY pleased with Nathan Leonardo. Nathan Leonardo's fees were reasonable, he was extremely professional and compassionate about my defense. He was responsive to all my inquiries (and I had plenty). He communicated with me and included me in the entire process. To prepare for trial, he conducted research, hired an expert witness and requested maintenance/calibration results from the breathalyzer machine in an effort to better my position during the trial. And, during the jury selection, before the trial, Nathan included me in the process.

BOTTOM LINE...When a defendant is completely confident in their lawyer (like I was with Nathan Leonardo), the jury sees a confident team working together. I was found "not guilty". I recommend Nathan Leonardo highly. Your rights will be protected by a competent professional.

Outstanding Dedication and Tenacity

Mr. Leonardo is a man of outstanding dedication and tenacity. When I came to Mr. Leonardo with my DUI case, I was neither privy to the state laws nor the overall court proceedings. He helped educate me on the charges I was facing and the legal steps that would be taken with regards to such charges. Furthermore, I felt he was actually invested in the outcome of my case. Through Mr. Leonardo's tireless efforts and professionalism, my entire DUI case was dismissed without going to trial. If you need someone to fight for you in the legal system, Mr. Leonardo is the man for the job.

Honest, Fair & High Quality Attorney

Top notch legal expertise and advice! Mr. Leonardo was truly compassionate and professional in assisting me with my legal issues. I spoke to a few other attorneys and Mr. Leonardo was by far the highest qualified and the best. He is upfront, fair, and honest being a former federal litigator and member of the military. I felt comfortable speaking with him and believe he is a genuinely good person. I highly recommend him!!!

Highly Recommend

Mr. Leonardo did an excellent job representing me during my DUI case. With his help all my charges were dismissed during a jury trial. Without his help I would have probably accepted a plea bargain (jail time, license suspension, fines) but with Mr. Leonardo's help I decided not to and eventually got the charges dismissed. I would highly recommend his services.

He Cared

In all my dealings with him I felt that he cared about the outcome of my trial. I had complete trust in all his decisions. He was very knowledgeable and kept me informed and up to date on all incoming changes. I would not hesitate to hire him to represent me again if I ever need an attorney for any matter.

SPECIAL OFFER

As a token of my appreciation for your decision to purchase this book,[*] I am offering a complimentary, no-obligation legal strategy session for Arizona residents. This is a confidential, one-on-one session lasting up to forty-five minutes. During this session, we will discuss the facts of your case in person and devise a potential defense strategy.

To claim your free strategy session, simply call (520) 314-4125 and schedule *today*!

---

[*] If a friend or family member would also be interested in an absolutely *free* legal strategy session, have them call us today.

Made in the USA
San Bernardino, CA
23 March 2020